SMEOP

Published by Black Sunflowers Poetry Press, 2022
www.blacksunflowerspoetry.com

© Contributors 2022
Ed. Amanda Holiday
ISBN 978-1-7396267-0-9
All rights reserved

SMEOP
HOT

Contents

Radiant	5
Heat	17
Flames	35
Fire	53
Ablaze	67
Burning	79
Embers	89
Poets & Acknowledgements	101

RADIANT

Wind

Sing from the back
of your throat, out each nostril. Flare
in retention, bone beyond cartilage.

Smoke fills our lungs;
ceremony. Deep tones,
towards the fire and back, tabaco released
from palm toward each direction, we circle
round. Serpents
tongue the sky, lick for moisture, north,
rain; mosquitos. We are
not the only dancers.

Coral webbings, single hooves, paddles,
flips, stubs, only distant
memories of legs, dwell in my ear, vibrate,
dip down to root tap.
River through my canyon. Bead my brow.

Plants rattle to
the ground, seed pods wither and
burst; dry, sinking in, sought soil,
tunneling to fire. Perfume
of the body, we kiss by smelling.
Renewed, leaving
dried on skin, marking
shared territories, marred skin,
pores flooded, without wounding
(those are other rituals, fire-tipped,
of piercing and pulse).

I take you in by breathing
through
each motion,
deeper into emptiness, full
feathers flap, down my back
this place the clouds have hidden.

Seeded.

Snow falls

into the fire.

We mist up,
and grace the sky.

Ahimsa Timoteo Bodhrán

prayer that might unlock magic

heavenly father / absentee and incarcerated /
bless this offering of / almost human /
livestock too charred / to be enlightened /
and deliver / amethyst hailstorms /

forgive us / worshipping /
stoop scholars / gab grifters /
loose women / clenched boys /
unfurl in blood / always darker than / i remember /
bloodstone kingdoms / neck-knee /

evangelicals / spitting /
blue testament / indigo intolerant / asphalt scripture /
swallowed sermons / calcite bracelets /
rite reciting / miranda's elegy /
forgive us /

wild windpipes / chugging /
rose quartz / spitting / cyanide /

black magic / is only for /
immolating / bodies / we cannot inhabit

Joshua Moncure

Guabancex Falls In Love

I hurl to you   wild
   fire   escopeta   sin pudor
      no   pido   permiso
pa qué   your   forest
      stood   no chance
   los   animales   soy
      los   animales   roja
pelúa   testaruda   calcificada
   dentro   de   la   tierra
I run to you   igneous   terrain
      not asking   not holding back
  beating   tough   silvestre
      con las alas   de los buitres
    eating   flesh—just   your
      taste   my mouth
a moth   let me   fill it   with
   broken   wings   you
carry   shield   pa qué
     this flesh   can devour
   fluttering   just   let me
I crawl to you   goddess
   chewing   rot   spitting
     your name

Nicole Arocho Hernández

The Scent of My Words

The scent of my words
burning for you
smoke spirals perfume
mountain laurel and wolfsbane
belladonna and cedar cauldron flame.

If I were a witch I could concoct
more than a story—
of bleeding hearts laughing longing eyes lonely roads
ivy walled houses hiding riderless horses and unbuckled boots—

Come, love, come this night,
old flames we shall renew—
I'll set out the brightest stars
to mark the way for you—
over each fence
and past pestilence
a way for you to come through—

Where hearth coals are left to burn
a soft sheet music aflame,
and you would learn to scent
these words which I now name.

Olivia Lee

Pews

Catholicism / the comfort
of prayer / tactile
on wood / and red cushion
and all mothers / give bodies
to bring us here / Misericordia
mother / why must there be tears
and blood / for birth?
Who / proclaimed
this way / to wisdom?
And when priests / take a knee
and mothers / rise up
to the altar / to preach
will it be oral / or ovular
seminal / like semen
and seminary / or something
sacred / and ordinary?

Cassie Premo Steele

Penelope Prophesies at the Intersection of Phlox and Terra Pinguis

ένα (1 - éna)

Helio is hot he's always hot always will be hot
    so you better keep your distance, because it is not just
that his brilliance is blinding. He is an illusion. Even if you
    know it—even then—you might get carried away
in the summer.
In the summer he beams from 93 million miles away,
    and that is as far as he will ever be.
In the summer it is easy to miss those important details
    you ought to know, but by the time you do

it is autumn and already too late. Your disappointment
    descends like a tinted slough, the shed of dead leaves.
In autumn the entire universe seems like an illusion: you wonder
    if you can trust anything or anyone ever again.

δύο (2 - dío)

Helio is hot he's always hot always will be hot
    and you better beware when he circles in, because then
his brilliance will blister you. That is, when he touches you.
    You will feel the danger then, regard his glinting flint—
in the winter.
In the winter Helio moves 3 million miles closer
    and starts giving you the side eye.
In the winter he gives you the cold stare.
    The angle of your orbit changes,
        and   he   spreads   his   heat
  across   everything   and   everyone.

In the winter you will feel his heat ignite
    almost 10,000 degrees Fahrenheit, but you will shiver
like last summer when you thought Helio loved you
    but then you realized it was just a summer fling.

When spring swings around you will warm up to him again,
    feel the gravity of this   thing.
In spring you will see how it will always be
    with you and Helio. Like me, you'll proclaim it—

τρία (3 - tría)

Helio is hot he's always hot always will be hot
        and our love will last   forever.

I will love Helio
        every summer....   I will loathe him
                                              every winter.

Lisa Kamolnick

Hummingbirds in the Forest of Needle and Blood

Say there is a boy in a village. Say the boy is not always a boy, but today he is. Say he is wandering by cactus, not wanting to be stuck by thorns, but wanting to smell the flowers and gather the fruits, not on each leaf, because he is not greedy, but rather enough to feed himself and his people. Say the boy is stuck by thorns and begins bleeding, gets worried, gets lost, gets stuck by more thorns. Say the boy collapses, exhausted, and he is not sure where his tears end and the blood begins. Say he is crying, and the sound echoes through the forest of nopal. Say the wind carries that sound to another boy, a boy whittling wood, sharpening stones. Say that boy drops what he is doing, and picks them up again, ties them with leather, and goes searching for that voice. Say that boy hurries, and he is pricked by thorns. Say that boy begins bleeding, and crying, but keeps moving through the forest of thorned ovals and red fruit, each heart glistening with its own blood. Say the boy begins to echo the first voice with his own, weaving it, tying it with leather. Say each boy gets louder, but they are still separated by walls. Say each boy is frantic, crying, trying to reach the other. Say the walls are covered with blood. Say the walls get thinner, thornier, and one hand grasps another. And the cactus is just a sheath of breath, leather between two hearts, raon-raon-light, colibrí-quick. Say the boys slow down till they can find an opening in the wall, crack they can leverage, space they can push their bodies through. Say there will be more blood, more tears, more cactus between them. Say it will not matter. Say the second boy will bind the wounds of the first boy with leather, wood to splint his leg, stone to dig out any thorns. Say the first boy will feed the second some fruit, blot his blood with petals, dust his cheeks and chest with pollen. Say the second boy will bind their wrists with leather, not too tight, but enough to keep them from getting lost. Say the first boy will place their things in his basket. Say the second boy will grab a stick to keep them walking. Say they keep walking. Say they keep bleeding. Say they keep crying. Say they leave the forest of needle and blood. Say they return to this place, again and again, and gently touch each leaf. Say the wind keeps their story. The ground, their stories. Say their descendants keep returning, generation after generation, to gather fruit, make offering of pollen, point to the place of dried red-brown on green-pricked leaves, higher up on the branches each year, leave some leather, newly cut, some stones, newly polished. Say the blood we drink from each fruit is their own. Say this is story. Ours.

Ahimsa Timoteo Bodhrán

HEAT

The Poet Gets Advice from Tom Wolfe at Toscanini's Ice Cream Shop

A hundred degrees in Cambridge today:
a living heat that licks the melting crowds—
like cheap popsicles they seep and drip. Cafes
abandoned to the searing sun—no clouds
in sight—their chairs too hot for summer skin:
Bartley's Burgers' sidewalk tables stand bare
where a limp musician plays his violin—
the wilting notes condense and disappear.
The door to Toscanini's sweats and beads,
so cool it is inside where sweetness chills
the air. A dozen flavors today, I read.
Then, dressed in white from head to toe, he smiles
and whispers, "Try the Earl Grey Tea." It's new
to me. But he is he. And so I do.

Christina Lovin

Restrictions

The lawn is lemon-yellow, a knee of the house, not scraped but sunburnt, tight. No words can recall its Florida winter, those choices between cold and wet. *I don't care if I get fined*, my mother says, and puts her finger to the mouth of the hose to fan the hot water over her collection of spider plants.

At night I can hear the crickets watching me, posed weightless on the leaves. They do not breathe, nor do I, nor do we sleep. The back yard holds its breath, silent, not hot, but dark.

The brass rim of the hose burns my thigh, leaves a pink welt, like a kiss. I want to hold it over my head and let it flow down my neck, down my shirt, but I am afraid. I feel the hose stiffen. With just one squeeze from my hand, it would burst.

The umbrella tree loses its leaves first, the yard is littered with its beached canoes. Then the palms. My mother pulls the oranged fronds from the crowded trunk, her brown shoulders growing large and square. *I don't know how much longer I can take this*, she says, drinking from the hose, which she's left running all morning, the water pooling around her ankles.

Celia Alvarez

The Tempering

      i.

Evening, he laments the day's
small losses, robins in his voice,
trilliums in the damp woods.
Winter, he dispenses
antique remedies,
apothecary jars and quaint
urinals. The moon's an ember
in the sky, and the elms
are nearly blue with waiting.

      ii

He comes for the crackle
and spit of pine, smells smoke
drifting toward the kitchen
window, open a crack.
On the wall: *Old doctors
never die. They just lose
their patience.* His legacy:
beakers of urine, of sacred
semen, tinged red as coals.

      iii

High in the hills, the other side
of the river, *tools, all kinds.*
Among the saws and scythes
he brandishes a file, good one,
long and rough, no rust.
Held by his patient, one
he'd tried to save, and failed.
He pays for the tool,
cupping the widow's glad hand.

That night he lights a fire,
aged maple, and apple
stored in the tool shed.
It smolders till dawn

       iv

A three-year-old
hefts a log onto the blaze,
knees on the hearth
in pitchy jeans. Small hands
toughen on the bark
of fir, poke coals,
caving logs till they
shudder with sparks.
On the lake, mallards startle.

Hatchet in hand
children learn the art
of splitting kindling,
crisp wedges falling,
sweet sword fern at their feet.
Dust of triumph.

       v.

The woods glow, twigs
buried in a mulch of ochre
needles. Soon we will feed
even his bones to flame.

Carol Barrett

Sunday

Kept in ice
block twenty
thousand one leagues
beneath surface
opened sea
stinging closed
unseeing if
movement were
choice first
get to surface
second melt
it takes a while
none of it
is pleasant
kept at least
from crush
implosion
so to speak

Alex Starr

the languid way the air moves still as you wade in

heat I keep thinking of you
in a hat w/a tan watering the
grass & the utterly casual way
you suggest splashing w/me
through mud puddles to cool
off

Constance Bacchus

Spring

Today I found a smiley face baked into the ground
Dressed in fez or crown, ringed with wild
radish blossoms, cream colored crucifix simplicity
the very earthy opposite of passionflower's
complex trinity, dressed in purple velvet.
Today I saw a *duchifat* sitting in a tree
Kente cloth wings and hammer-head   she was not
where she was meant to be
but further down the wadi, another
chopsticked her way across the dirt.
It's already too hot in the sun some days,
and the green is paling golden.
Summer is nearly here.
Spring is fleeting.

Both my boys are shaving.

Lisa Namdar Kaufman

Lighter Reds, Fading Blue

I've switched my route to graffiti where
storefronts would drop
spiked blends to laced Wellies. What you take?
warped to where you at? real quick. How often
have I gauged force wrong. One in five stops
at a child blindfolded with a mirror
not to be seen, the way zero say something
with the same zipped stillness I hoped it was nothing—
a foreman a few weeks back
tossing bones like beams in a pile.
I was carrying bougainvillea like they were
lilacs in a vase, to the crypt.
My great-greats understand
I grow no shade, rain or shine. And take
no cover. The stenciled waif sheds chalk.
This hot, how do kids still shoot out on a lawn
even if it's paint
or water. It would take more than
an art to get me cracking. To forge from verge.
I was more a pills person, out like a light three days,
how an embryo might slumber on
to fetus or succumb.
Who wants to know? soon to get lost in
who isn't the city? Here is that ash on my fingertip.
Chrysanthemum in hand. My head still damp
in a towel, same threadbare rag
for a small fire.

Kris Falcon

Sun Drip

Sherbet sun drip
onto this surface
structure encrusted
your fiery dome's
day pool sticky sweet
sea breeze flaps
face flicks
fringe as a furzy
towel freshly hung
to dry even smog
is too lazy to bear
down with its brown
tongue chessboard
cement cracks
under stress of life's
breath smoky sung
surly tongued
spitting its sailor's
language animate
the zephyr still sky sir
with your soundless departure
crocodiles are not fond
of crocs flesh yes
shade beckons sexing
sweat wrestles across
bridge of brow
clumsy combatants
swollen with sticky sweetness
laborious fruits of unlabor
all along the western front
he even clogs four
bullet holes in him

Alex Starr

Fall in Miami

The heat rises from the pavement
just as it has all year, and the women
sitting at the bus stop are just as wilted.

There were no leaves on the trees
to begin with. There is no sense
of a cycle. It is endless summer,

and, like all curses, no one
remembers wishing for it.
Soon there will be Christmas

trees for sale, pyrotechnic pines
yellow and thinning as old hair.
The tourists will descend like

buzzards, picking at what's already
dead, boasting loudly about how
this time last year they had to shovel

six feet of snow off the front porch.
The natives will dance around them
and flare their skirts like hungry whores.

I will sit in my small, air-conditioned
room and wonder what it's like
to close my eyes and feel that cold.

Celia Alvarez

California Sunday

California Sunday
Trade my sunglasses
For a portrait of the sky.

Typical place to call my own,
The matted hair for a ceiling,
Crumpled fist for a light socket.

Three times I ask when to
Call, each ring has no answer.
No fight to my voice, so I'm glad.

A couple Mid-Western Winters
Will put me in my place,
I'm sure that's all it'll take.

Sweet eyes, sour heart.
A couple broken ones is
All it takes, I guess.

Daniel Peralta

strings attached

Canopy ties above my head -
    three strings attached to a bamboo pole
    and shade to cover my light skin.

Small hen in my freezer that I forgot to thaw last night –
    round bowl, warm water creating more of a pool
    or whatever than I've ever had.

Lucky fucking hen.
Dead. Warm. Soaking.

Daniel Peralta

July

July is the time of yellow and black hovering
over salvia and bellflower
wandflower like a cluster of magenta mist
ragged-edged poppies & puddles
(the afterthought of storms)
as dragonflies flash over pond
carrying light in their stained glass wings
as hummingbirds slice humid air
en route to hover & sip
from hibiscus petals like scarlet bowls.

In July spiderwort high as my hips
droops & burns in afternoon sun
rich brown roads that seemed amaranthine
in June now run grey & end in hills
long before horizon
tall grasses that once threatened
to pierce clouds bow meekly behind guard rails
the gods of crocus & iris have gone
leaving only mute remnants of chalice petals
rotting in dry ground.

I traipse through my garden in July
trying to accept the inevitable decline of lilies
stark & decapitated
while monarchs grace larkspur & skim sage
water hyacinth ferry their purple pikes
idly across patina'd ponds
stirred by a wind promising a storm
that will darken road & horizon
then leave petal & grass dripping & humming
my garden a singing bowl.

Taunja Thomson

Swimming Lessons

At seven, the early part of summer was spent learning
        to swim in a pool where the water only came up to my chest.

I cheated. I never took my feet off the bottom.
        The Atlantic, a different story, so huge

I stayed on shore making shapes in the sand.
        Camp counselors tried to coax me in. Failing,

they seized my arms and legs, carried me
        as far as they could and threw me towards the waves.

I hit the water and sank. When instinct or instruction
        kicked in, I swam for the shimmering, golden glow

beyond the surface. Life is just as terrifying as learning to swim,
        and I can't see the light beyond the murkiness,

but I've learned it's not the tide that kills
        the drowning; it's the terror-filled struggle.

I want to stop struggling against the universe,
        so much bigger than an ocean. When I'm going under,

I want to surrender and allow what is within to lift me
        on to the waves and carry me to shore.

Ellen June Wright

Familiar with the Moment

1.

Day lilies explode from every corner
of the garden: jazz hands, bugles.
Pretend we are the only ones here, all
that matters, even in a world where all is
ephemeral and teetering, we have you beat.

2.

According to those familiar with the moment
much was said and nothing substantial.
Everything unuttered hung in the spaces
like overripe fruit that would fall soon
for lack of picking – wasted, decomposing.

3.

It's too hot to sleep, too late to turn
on the bedside lamp to write down the lines
you've composed that seem to have substance.
Kid yourself you will remember in the morning.
Kick off the sheet; recover yourself.

4.

June never remembers how quickly
September arrives. Make your lists, go
to the farmer's market, imagine anew that this
will go on and on, every moment well-used,
that you won't soon feel cheated, unfruitful.

Sharon Dornberg-Lee

Storm Coming

Just before daybreak I hear cannons
        blast open the sky. Hairs on my arms

and neck stand erect, and I remember
        the last storm and how for the first time

I feared being alone. Transfixed, I sat
        until I gathered the courage to hide under

the covers. Again, I wait for what feels like
        Judgment. Like the antediluvians, I've learned

it's too late to think of building storm
        shelters when I hear the thunder coming.

Ellen June Wright

FLAMES

Red-burning

one tulip stretches its fibrous stem through a barberry hedge
to a gravel driveway on the other side

    read a bit of Wanda Coleman
    get with her Real lingo-resilience
    2 minutes I swing imagining

spring concludes her time with petal fall—

    my lasso lashes tight   traps—whatever it Licks/

    Likes says Okay

    ThursdayJupiterJesus—ColdStayNoMore

    #@Home-with-The-Poem:

    one burning cup

    I want Someone to Touch

Gail Langstroth

Soft Machine (Holiday)

Meet me again in some heat,   sweatdriven living   repeatedly ruined as we go on inside some new opinion,   second Sunday afternoons where nothing shines &   heavy is too heavy to be made less away from bed. You_blue as a brand-new hotel room,   brothers fight between   floor & sofa-bed as   parents slip into   ound of air conditioning unit, no more real than   place itself, rather; *recycled;* memory bitter like   handfuls of candy   forget line our pockets. Me– I'll standby- amber light of almost, waiting for Love on   balcony wearing bedsheets like   TV tells,   un of somewhere caught over   strange fiction of   a Summer holiday. Us–   an urgent silver, we're sand inhabiting   rental car, sitting like an alligator in   community pool–Buddy The Lifeguard has more bullets than teeth, (save   day), we hunt chlorine until our eyes go redheavy, then navydamned, &   towels take us home.

I was lost down a washed-out road,   Southern thunder dismantling until   sky was only spare parts, highways empty, restaurants full. My brother faints from   spiderbite; waitress' arms around me counting freckles until   fries arrive   finally remember my name. I talk about home; where rain is   shy, where ambulances don't   cry, where you count hairs left on a dandelion clock wishing   Summer back inside.

Thomas Irvine

Suspicion

When the upstairs neighbor knocked on my friend's door and told him his car was on fire, they walked over to the window together to confirm, a silent and strange moment since they had never spoken before and he hadn't had a woman alone in his apartment for ages and then the police were suddenly there taking details for the report so neither exchanged much personal information and yet in the weeks that followed after the car was towed, after the insurance claim filled, after he had bought a red Vespa and zipped around dark corners in town, something about their shared-secret smiles in the hallway led him to slip a note under her door one morning, which led to a night together doing clay face masks in her tiny bathroom, a courtship, an elegant wedding on the Cape, a house, a brindle bulldog, a son with red hair, and now in their second decade together, my friend and I sit on my porch with ice in our old man Scotch whiskeys and he asks me quietly and for the first time if I think it's possible she set the car on fire just so she could talk to him.

Stephanie Staab

Sugar

Sugar yOu're in heels but
just barely reach my moUth
dress coated on you like monochRome frosting

still sunshine on (the day beFore) the hottest day of the year
first thinking *how close should* I *stand* before later making love
over whetheR
it'S better to burn alive or drown,
The grooves of your eyes

growing darker and Deeper
As the last of our light clocked off in Soho
suddenly across The road- it's the 1920s and the war is
over! gimlEts all round;

yOu grabbed my hand
across the dark parts of an Underground bar,
bodies almost buckled into the otheR's-   *O Sugar* I'm

Folding, learning, loving to learn about you-
tonguestick into the sIlence of a liquor-
soaked maraschino cherRy,
thinking of the red that escapeS your lower lip
(and how I wish iT would meet my collar), before I got brave

and tieD the stem with my tongue—
bAby how did you do that?   open
your mouth and I'll Teach you,   let's
start anothEr war with the time we have left,   let's

end the wOrld to end an
evening with the most beautiful mUsic in a
century. If we sit any closeR we'll crash

so beFore
I pour you back into a cab
you let me in behind youR disposable mask
and slip me Something
sweetT

to take away on my homewarD
trAin, nursing your
Taste like hard candy
until it's corruptEd back into my own

Thomas Irvine

CLUB PARADISE Lost

One woman to one hundred forty-four
of them, the men: the odds of paradise
or that strobe-lit stage of limbo before?
The lovely devils levitate and writhe
in smoke, like Rodin's muscled multitudes
in hell. The halogen burns hot above
as I ignite below the glistening rood.
On borrowed wings he hovers, smooth-skinned dove.
His wing tips brush my body like the holy sigh
he presses to my ear: "Nine inches that
will make you scream my name..." And I,
my tongue struck dumb, my breath *magnificat,*
but where (although I cannot speak his name)
I touch his shining horn, my fingers flame.

Note: Club Paradise is a gay strip club in Cambridge, MA

Christina Lovin

Lessons for Fifty Cents

I learned how to make love
watching the lions in the Seattle zoo
on weekends in the afternoon
sun, smelling of popcorn and peanuts.
They talk all the while, screaming
in the mount, bringing the masses
of their bodies together in jubilant
choreography, pushing every giant muscle
into oblivion. They ignore timid
observers (Catholics after church)
come from another continent altogether.
For hours, they show off for multitudes
of peeled jackets and instamatic cameras.
If Daddy knew what I was doing
there, he would have been quite
proud (Pittsburgh has a lovely zoo.)*

That is why I am
a little noisy, don't care
if someone sees us, explosions
of movement are with me all afternoon.
Stretched out in my heat,
outrageously demanding –
it is all a matter
of how you're taught.

*So does San Diego.

Carol Barrett

The Fine Line Between Transcendence and Impropriety

Making love with windows open
Sneaky breeze our messenger
Cries and screams
Out and in
Outward and inward
    Motor groan straining
    Schoolchildren chirping
    Your unclothed demand the neighborhood know pleasure
When I no longer could distinguish now from then
Famished claws pierced my shell
We knew we had arrived somewhere worth revisiting

                                                            MK Punky

Lady Godiva's Glance

Lady Godiva wore wings
sharpened at the ends

& rode her long brown hair
throughout the town.

At 50, her face was wide & sly
& her wrinkles glimmered

in sun—torso & arm & neck.
Leofric had commented on them

often enough. In the end
he lowered the taxes

embarrassed as he was
by her bare limbs

bumpy nipples
& the fire

that blazed
in her glance.

Taunja Thomas

ECCE FEMINA

I am the woman whose
Hair is on fire.

I'm screaming:
"Help! My hair!"

Passersby do look
My way.

Some of them nod.
Some of them say:

"There goes a woman whose
Hair is on fire."

Then they keep looking
Away.

Peggy Landsman

How I Want To Be Wanted

after Henri Rousseau – The Dream, 1910

That man who painted me nude in his Paris studio
and later seduced me on a velvet divan—
he was no kind of match for his lions and snakes.
I missed being ravished by wildness.
In the end, I dreamed myself back
to the rain forest, to those tropical snakes
so inflamed by my beauty they had to be soothed
by a flute player while they writhed into shapes
that mimicked my hips, my breasts and my thighs.
That's how I want to be wanted—
with the type of desire the lions had for my throat.

Laura Ann Reed

My Unlikely Self-Portrait

        sable brush strokes swiped
against Revlon red
        exultant undulations
licorice-lace limbs   jive-jointed,
        heavy-hipped   bold-bellied
arms held high   lithe hallelujahs
        lickety flick split
in serendipitous harmonious sin-
        you-us tongue tied   dance[1]

---

[1] Note to biographers: you will not recognize me in this va-va-voom version, this fauvist fling.[2]

[2] You might not either, love, although you are the backbeat drummer, loose-letter, timekeeper, the painter, the brush, color, canvas, and frame.

Jeanne Julian

A Burning

Without so much as a saying-so look, smallest
fraction of a tilt of the head –
but in that pause,
that slowly glow-ripening space
between one sentence and a whole new life time,
there was the beginning: in this uncoupling
of normality from the cast off selves
we'd so separately been. – You heard it too,
your pause, our growing;
the invisible gap between us closing,
even as you opened your mouth to let the next words fly free
and found them gone already,
touching my lips
before leaving yours, or both, or something entirely
new that pulled your eyes after, burning the moment
to ashes
in a rush of lost time.

You swallowed.
I blinked.
Mid-lecture and in a fully witnessing auditorium –
but we both knew there was no cold amount
of now or future water
would ever quell this, totally.

Angela Arnold

We carry our identity on our fingertips

When you think that I'm not looking,
you bring your fingers to your nose.
We carry our identity on our fingertips,

you say, *pattern recognition-based,*
all those whorls and arches.
I'd know them anywhere, baby,

your ridges, and loops,
how fiercely they grip and throttle.
Tonight I slice the garlic, season the roast,

rub cinnamon, brown sugar, pepper
and salt into the meat.
Sear it evenly on all eight sides.

When I bring my fingers to my nostrils, I smell dinner;
when I bring them to yours, you smell love.
I watch you scrape those tasty bits

from the bottom of the pot,
deglaze with beef broth and merlot.
We tie the rosemary sprigs with twine;

float them above the nascent gravy,
chopped onions the crown on top.
You set the timer for 70 minutes,

program the Instant Pot for quick release.
Meanwhile, in the bedroom, we've got time.
You school me in the efficacy

of facial recognition, palm prints, iris I.D.
rub your body all over mine, finger my flesh,
program me for quick release.

Alexis Rhone Fancher

If French Kissing Was as Good as Promised, Shouldn't I be Happy by Now?

I am accidentally thinking
about snail sex when we start. Mouths open.
Tongues. When snails have sex
there is a slightly gruesome amount of suction.
      First, a tingling graze of eye stalk on eye stalk.
      Then a lack of movement. Wet flesh. Fireworks.
Outside my neighbor is walking his Husky home.
Cicadas grate their stiff wings.
My refrigerator clicks on like a drunk uncle
wandering into church mid-mass. Snails
keep going at it for hours, tonguing each other
with their whole foot. Briefly I imagine your tongue & slime.
Briefly I imagine peanut M&Ms
spilling from our lips, more than we could hold in our mouths,
rolling everywhere like runaway sleds.
      After you leave, I sweep the peanut M&Ms outside.
      The blue jays get sugar high & riot.
Snails shoot calcium love darts. Snails pull each other
out of their own private viscosity.
They are in the open. They ignore the circling hawks.
      We tuck our tongues in. We walk away.

Emmy Newman

Burning the Love Letters

Regret nothing that has brought you joy—
    ephemera or solid flesh:

they are those lovers and their words
    that aroused you with their weight.

Lament instead the mad rash loss
    of proof that you have been desired.

Christina Lovin

FIRE

Dead Space

i sold black power,
        fist over palm over
                fist. rocket fuel is not

cheap, and black
        dreams are gas guzzling.
                there goes another ounce

again, i fall for you
        straight across atlantic
                sized blunts you roll.

blunt is how love
        prefers to smoke me.
                behind three closed eyes &

a three/fifths clenched jaw
        rattling words like, why
                are you playing dead?

save the dramatics
        for the bedroom, expired
                tags aren't as dangerous

as the look in your
        eyes. officers are newborn
                soft. are you trying to scald?

white flags don't stay
        white when they forget
                to flap & fold & wave

their flesh as a target.
        calm down and let me
                do the talking, this time

your lungs are taking
        off too quickly, your last
                trip isn't over & done.

with a smile & some
        sunscreen, space-walks
                are simple as bullseye.

Joshua Moncure

Missing Some Blue in the Green

The city has no yard. A boy learns to play
a song with glasses of water, a spoon.
To sound like a xylophone if he can't like the ocean.
When nothing trickles from a drum
or the sky, he drinks his wells. Before any turns
vapor or wine he empties until
he hears his voice. Tiny pool, drop of a cent.
Maybe it's as close as he can be. Here's to prayers
for elsewhere, to be someone else, even
from a carrier of the new lethal running
for shade, crushing mimosa.
Slowing the world down.
Clouds will not shift back to shape.
Who has faced the ask for otherwise
cannot help but bargain. Runners up
who do not see through the end watch,
mute behind tinted forts. Every night is
an all-nighter, burning where it does not add up.
Lenders who count on no visit
flower a path though they can cut to any corner,
no snag. A lot of using goes on as much as good.
Dreamers who sleep all day
sleep through the first audit. A blistered palm
finds moss along the ramparts. To cushion
a fall? How many shortcomings in a setback?
But it is getting easier embracing
abstract, the town pantry full,
loving like an aunt or brother. Then like a son,
a rival, the other end of a transceiver, so on,
a bully with his arm left to twist.

Kris Falcon

REQUIEM FOR LAKE STREET, MINNEAPOLIS, MAY 28 2020

> *God's fate*
> *Is now*
> *The fate of tress, rocks, sun and moon*
> *Yehuda Amichai*

Fate took a beating last night:
Knee crushing the neck, eyes
Torn by gas, the medieval
Cackling of old wood, afire.

A tree of thick black smoke
Rises from the street, thick wooden
Beams its roots, every bit of air
Sucked up into scream. An older

Mexican woman stands in front
Of her shattered glass, shaking
Her head. Bits of morning fall
From her hair like lit cigarettes.

There is no loneliness left to share.
This path, first traveled by deer and
Bear, under a sibilant moon; then came
The Lakota, stitching the Great

River to the chain of Lakes. Swedes,
Norwegians, Somalis, Hmong. All
Followed the trail. But this thick morning,
Only a small Bobcat rumbles towards

The piles of charred wood, one siren
Screams at another, and a helicopter
Pummels the rising Sun, the vanishing moon,
The stars with their hands over their faces.

Patrick Hansel

Aquiver

      Papa, why wouldn't the wolf just leave them alone?
     They were peaceful piggies,   weren't they?
They didn't fight   back,   they used their words &
             their brains like me right?
  Papa, where were all the grownups?
They,   they   should've   done something!

Did the wolf have
  little brothers & little sisters? Maybe they
         might've been friends
              with the piggies?
   Maybe the piggies
even knew the three bears. Yup,
    they got bothered too! Their breakfast, & their chairs, & their beds!
But I know it's just a story, in real life Goldilocks' parents would see her going away
    & run to   save her.   Next time,
Goldilocks should listen to the little
voice inside her head   that was saying: *no,* *thank you,*
I'll stay here, safe *with my grown-ups.*
    Papa
     did her parents forget to tell her? or did,
   they want her
     to get lost?

         My dear boy, again
       awake before the whippoorwills,
wild-eyed, throat aquiver.
      My palm,   smoothing your furrowed brow.
    Thumb caressing the cowlick above your widow's peak.
I promise you,   again:
     Thunder is just the night's belly
       tumbling & rumbling & bumbling— Yes,
there's no lightning, & even if there was—that's right, we're safe on the 1st floor.
              —But— Papa,
is Pharaoh still dead?/
     I can't remember all the plagues
from the puppet show in school/ but
     I learned Egypt has toy stores now! & a Downtown
     With buildings like mine in Chicago/ Yup! Egypt even has
  trains now/ But not
     like the Underground   Railroad/

```
Because people walked                              for that  train/
        Papa,         Black    people
          can go anywhere!
                              we can ride the bus!!/
        I like the big window way, way,    way in the way back/
                                                        they can't
    take      us
                    to jail like Rosa Parks/ or the Doctor
                    & the Reverrinmartin Luther King Junior.      Nope!/
        But, wait, uhm, are,
                    are the girls      still
                    dead    who were       in the church?/
            What games    were they playing?/  Papa, did they all share the toys?/
Did their grown-ups,
                cry          for a long time?/


Papa, the puppet show said    Pharaoh killed his son/           I just wonder,
                    how           he did it?


            No, no,      no!    Let's    not talk about that anymore.
    I don't really think
                    grown-ups would forget  their kids,
                unless magic                              made them.
I saw the news           paper.
        Those kids in the    shiny    sparkle    blankets     were    sleeping
        on the floor/         I didn't see any grownups
                                            inside the fence with them/
        The person holding the camera
didn't go                          find their grownups!
            All the  bunk beds
                    are      still      empty.
                You said
                    kids need
                        lots of sleep     to grow
        But Papa
            I got woke
                    up too
                    early
                                    by the storm.
        Can you
        slide over?


                                        Saleem Hue Penny
```

ZOOM

ZOOM....

ZOOM UP

OPEN YOUR MIC AND BE SUBMITTABLE

SMILE AND PROTEST YOUR METAPHOR

BREAK OFFLINE

READ THE DAILY BEAST BREAD

THE WRITING AND THE KNOWING

FUCK THE IMPORTANCE OF IMITATION

WORKSHOP YOUR HONEST SOLITUDE

YOUR EXAMINATION OF TERMINOLOGY

YOUR DECOLONIZING

YOUR EXPERIENCE THAT'S WELCOMED

AND NOTHING'S EVER DUE.

Alprentice X Aries

From Paris Hilton's DVD Collection

Too Hot to Handle

The Long, Hot Summer

Cat on a Hot Tin Roof

The Hot Spot

Last of the Red Hot Lovers

Hot Tub Time Machine

Mama June: From Not to Hot

The Hot Chick

Some Like It Hot

Hot Mess Millionaire

Janis Butler Holm

The Naughtiest Dirtiest

When we had our friends Jasmine and Tiffany over for dinner and board games
after Boggle and Pictionary
we played one of those innocuously scandalous truth-or-dare type contests
with cards and dice
as a welcome distraction from our ongoing conversation
about systemic racism in America
a subject our Black lesbian guests understood in ways we never could

Jassy landed on a square that entitled her to draw a card
which promised five points if she'd reveal her naughtiest dirtiest sex fantasy
and an extra five if her wife had written down the same debauchery

They both laughed with an endearing snort
flashing their lover a knowing confirmation

That one's too easy
they said almost simultaneously
we both pretend we're white males

MK Punky

For Jim who Thinks We Need More Cops

You normally hide in your husk jimmy-jim-jim
When the producer says lights/camera/ action/
You usually speak directly into the mic on your
bright-red Armani tie with key points for the blue-color
layman to cheer.
 jimmy-jim-jim you never fail to surprise
The interviewer asked if we need fewer cops-
You vehemently reply: no-in fact-we need more!

More!

jim why do we need more?
Don't you feel safe & bullet-proof
in your husk that moves like
a tank-led cavalcade, proclaiming
victory over heathenism?
Know you feel safe when you
can see-hear dixie climb from
the antebellum throngs of Civil-War
recreators who wave with an
esoteric wave/ grab the hands
of the kids on their shoulders
and train-program them
to do the same...
Again jim, why do we need more cops?
Don't you feel safe in your
husk that sounds like a plantation/
bleeds like a massacre/
buries & reproduces/
just to repeat the same jig--
Don't you feel safe enough in your husk, eating pecan
pie Sipping mammies breast milk from the family's
silver plated decanter set-
tapping your feet while *all-the brown* babies suffer
from diabetes/*tennessee* whiskey/
and the weary blues--
in your husk the *weary blues*
rock you to sleep & you never-ever
worry about anything-
not even being apologetic
& redundant--
or should i say: unapologetic
And not giving a fuck-

Durrell Thompson

JIMMY CANT SLEEP

Jimmy Jacob Roberts, twenty years
sober from booze, and twelve
from smack, shows up at my door
on Maundy Thursday, having been
up seventy-two hours, drinking,
smoking crack, taking speed,
planning to kill his girlfriend,
the third one in a row
he picked up at AA, the third
one in a row who dumped him
and his neediness onto the sidewalk.

He wants my opinion as a pastor.
He wants to borrow money—
"just to get some coffee". He wants
to cry, to tell me he still loves her,
to tell me he's going to kill her,
God help him, "Is it wrong
to ask for forgiveness before
you do something, pastor?"

Good Friday 3 am: he bangs on
my door, demands wisdom and cash.
Easter morning: 5 am, he sleeps
on the mat in front of that door,
arms curled as if holding the child
he was born into. I have to step
around him to get to the corner deli
and break my Lenten fast.

When I come back, he is gone.
I don't know if he pounded on my door,
I don't know if he cursed at me
through the darkness. I don't know
if he killed that girl. I just know
that he will be back tonight,
on my steps or in my dream,
and that I will not know
what to do with him

                                        Patrick Hansel

ABLAZE

Fire Crew

My kids are off fighting fires while I water
My raspberries. Back on furlough, they tell me
Of back burns and clouds of beetles that flutter
Into the blaze to lay eggs. They love the hierarchy,
The old-timers razzing the fresh recruits
About tools and pant cuffs. Everything they do
Is wrong, but they're learning—the NATO alphabet
The speed at which the green blackens, how a crew
Comes together. Puffy with poison oak,
They swig beer and talk excitedly of their next
Tour. I watch them share inside jokes
With envy. If I were younger, I expect
I'd follow them to where a day's work mattered
Rather than dither over which bushes I've watered.

Devon Balwit

The Frog in the Water Set to Boil

When Los Angeles began to burn
fulfilling the predictive model constructed by annoying scientists
whose shrieking warnings periodically interrupted our favorite entertainments
we noticed the unbreathable air
the wildlife gasping on our dying lawns
the apocalyptic gloom obscuring the sky
but we were far too busy
hating each other
to do anything about it

MK Punky

Wildfires

that year when the smoke came
i reached for a ball of yarn on the ground
but it rolled away

i kept the other end of the thread
in my pocket where it felted into a
nice thick stick i sometimes used to stir my tea

there were seven days but on the sixth
we knew there would never come a seventh
because that would mean rest and we don't

the herbs spill over the yard
the oregano crosses the street
the neighbor will fuss
i don't know the neighbors
i worry i'll cross the street
and the oregano
won't know the seventh day either

i wait so long to follow the thread
it tugs for me
i see a bird tuck into itself to sleep and i go
the thread leads to a knot of multiple threads
extending out in all directions
others |like me| arrive
the tree rings narrow as the smoke clears
the burn mark seals this memory

big surprise the seventh day comes
i find my neighbor
she wants the oregano
a thread is tied to her ankle as she walks

apparently you can still give gifts
you can still give
you can

even as you rest

Corinne Hughes

Blame it on a Flower Moon

Let's plant a seed under shielded sky
       amid wild Valencia orange trees
       whose spheroid colors testify

adrift in a sea of palmetto mazes
       to make the point—soft globes, hard lines—

headily entwined in nature's embraces
       like thieves in tangles on a moonlit night.

Let's venture under the canopy
       among lush, magnificent live oak trees
       whose arms unfurl to steal the sky

where stars and moon conjoin astral phases
       with earthen Gods—hard ground, soft light—

as Cold Creek meanders in tender phrases
       like whispers flowing to a thirsty ear.

Let's wind our way through earth and sky
       along trails of honey-milked moon and trees,
       forget the several reasons why

lose ourselves in corporeal mazes—
       let go of should and should we not—

find ourselves in each other's gazes
       like vines entwined 'round a live oak tree.

Let's plant a seed under full moon's light—
       two souls in tune,
       one hope so near—

come harvest, find two hearts
       are three.

Lisa Kamolnick

Molten

a metal trellis leans toward the stone wall
I train roses to slip through its ornate lattice

yesterday, admiring thorns: small sailboats, miniature
Mount Fujis concluding in a bent red point, I cut a stem

for the thorns—not the rose

at my table-desk this morning, the one my friend Anita
found in Berlin's Charlottenburg, leaves stretched

legs cut for my writing height—
I hold my face in hands, elbow weight entrusted

to table's scarred oak—how much longer
before—burning cars, bullets, cops—

asphalt streets : our altar now
before hate—soothed to calm water

before fear & flaming—
how much needs to change

before Fujis are scaled—
& boats freed—full sail

what's the sense of thorn?

until we can kneel
chaos fumes sting—before

calyx-sepals
5-leafed

something like molten
stands—reborn

Gail Langstroth

Construction

The fire crowns beyond the limits.
We crawl through this city on the way
to work, shop, park, see a play.
A play of humanity, the small family
struggles to keep fed, find safe sleep,
silence the whine of sirens for the maimed
or dead. A crane poses to build more
structures that will fall down one day
when an end dwindles and good citizens
have run out of escape routes and shelters.
Fouled air paralyzes us or the earth
turns molten or liquifies. Now we pass
not thinking, continue daily in crowds
as time has always run from here to hereafter,
and that bit of after loiters on as work in progress.

Tricia Knoll

The Multiverse

> *"I was afraid of the dark because then I could see/Everything."*
> *Joy Harjo*

In dreams and fantasies, I visit other versions of our world.
In some, the sun's gone supernova, burnt out like a briquet
in a spent grill, or worse, nothing's left, just a blank gap,
where our planet, like a pulled tooth, used to be.
Everything we made is gone, our monuments and art,
acts of hope we dreamed would last forever. Some
new species we can't imagine dominates the world
we claimed. I shouldn't mind that. It's us I'm longing
to escape, our human urge to uproot all that's beautiful,
bulldozing ancient redwoods, building roads
where mountains used to rise.

Robbi Nester

Target Audience

Wipe out a species, with God at our side. —Harryette Mullen

but just two bugs on the wind
shield nephew fever rapid

rapid but smoke from Redding
to Weed & testing rapid

windshield odd but just two bugs
under just 2000 miles

negative bugs negative
rapid but bugs no bugs no

Jeanne Morel

Harvesting Thursdays

Saturday intentions, Sunday plans, blown fiery
up and apart: there, boom! A crater

where sensible hope should be spinning plans. –
A hole where dirty water will do *its* thing in no time.

Gone: the jagged edges, the singed, the serrated,
the splinters with their clear, clean voice of reason.

Gunk in the puddle of the waters
of life: rich slime and what might crawl from it

the only possible harvest. Though not
by Thurs(or any)day calendars offer by way of

meaning: the hanging by our common thread.
We, never-I, should have known, seen

our unresisting oceans dragged clean,
the forests cindered, planet tiger torn to scatters

among oil-drenched lands, home of a crushed billion
inundated, hungry people, revolving, with a last

drumming of heels on the good earth, noticeably (yes,
now) dying. – But we've bagged it all up, zipped

our mouths. And still count on another regular
Thursday: we named it, all but christened it.

We're owed it.

Angela Arnold

The Core
dir, Jon Amiel, 2003

was everything we wanted that night,
simply a virtuous team of genius scientists with a clear goal:
to drill into the Earth and save us all.
No ulterior plot points or villains or inexplicable love triangles,
a few mildly humorous mishaps in a ship building montage
(all easily fixed) in order for nuclear capabilities
to become the solution we've all been waiting for
to the worst thing: an unreasonable end.
The phallic ship sets out into its trajectory.
The team rigs bombs and start dying
regularly scheduled as baby teeth.
Like Borges and the perpetual motion machine,
revered for its unreproachable perpetuity despite
well-known futility to describe what manner of thing the world is,
the worst thing is forgetting the thinking machine
does not work. The worst thing is not packing snacks for a long car trip.
The worst thing is miscalculating the core temperature. The worst thing is isolation
without clear finalization. The worst thing is remembering how
summers used to be mild and winters bearable on the West Coast,
is understanding the cost/benefit analysis,
is believing that the whales will save us after all.

Emmy Newman

BURNING

Hell Planet

If they tell us one side is lava hot enough to vaporize rocks, you can expect
  the flip side is still cranking the big wheel of darkness. Magma will always
    remind you of the best birthday cake you were ever baked with the herd of plastic horses
        posed on it galloping across the chocolate field
and how some of the candles burned down to the horse bodies
    and dripped the molten plastic all over. It's important at times like
        the discovery of this Hell Planet to remember happening upon your high school crush
      sandwiched between two bookshelves with his shirt off. Your young arousal, him
    with his plaid boxers bunching over his running shorts, you
            pretending this was a normal classroom where you had come
      back to retrieve your normal
              forgotten notebook. I'm thinking yearbooks are a capitalist tool
            to monetize memory and you're thinking I'm right. I wish we had known
              about all those vaporizing minerals on the Hell Planet carried
          by the raging winds to rain rocks into the lava oceans
    instead of retaking school pictures with, and without the smile.
    Would you wish for a rock tornado to have a good summer?
On your visit to the World's Only Corn Palace, you can't bring Frisbees or alcohol
    so you replay the cross-country boys dancing in their red shorts last homecoming
      again and again in your head. No wonder you never kissed a boy in high school,
          stoppered up with too much wanting. You could make yourself squirm
      from a daydream in AP US History but it only made you worried about leaving
a wet mark from between your shorts on the plastic chair. At least on the Hell Planet
shorts have become irrelevant and anyway, I've heard he's a medical supply salesman now,
        your high school crush. I've heard all planets start molten.

Emmy Newman

Making the Best of Death

If you don't have hope, why bother? asks Goodall.
The acequias of NM are running dry, but you can still

find *Middlemarch* in a free box, annotated only
until page 5, the rest open for interpretation.

You can carry it to the cooling station, bon mots
flaring up like brush in dry forest. Allow

yourself to focus not on char, but
on the collaboration of firefighters,

gathering across a multitude of lines
to do what they can.

Even walking is a kind of falling.
You almost go down, but recover, making

your way where you're headed. Tourists
pose in the heat by a sign that reads 126°.

Look at them making the best of Death
Valley. You revisit the faith of your youth,

or a new faith, piloting your small copter
towards a blaze with your payload of water.

Devon Balwit

August Omens

Two crows sitting in the middle
of the road, black feathers gleaming
in the pale, pallid summer morning.

Later we will see turkey vultures
picking at the carcass of a small
animal: We turn our heads and
pretend not to see the signature
of death and decay smeared
and soldered on gravel.

Lazily gorging on this meager
meal, these creatures will rise
at sunset to circle over us as we
race each other down the high-
way, beckoning with rural hands
and whispering with rusted tongues.

The static heat of the Impending
hums and swells in intensity
like summer cicadas, and
the screaming multitude of
the Inevitable swarms into
our ears.

Jennifer Thal

The Rocking Horse of the Everyday Apocalypse

> *Everything flows, everything changes.*
> *You can't board the same prison train twice.*
> *Vasily Grossman*

Bears that are spotted in Lithuania generally come from Belarus

or Latvia
        & about those stuffed animals
at the winter Olympics—

On the bed beside me, poems by Milosz, the Polish poet
exiled on Grizzly Peak Boulevard in the Berkeley Hills,
robins, oaks, eucalyptus.

I spray the houseplants for ants
we are all implicated
I pull words from here

What are the moral implications of collage or juxtaposition-?
I place them
there

When I go to sleep, it's silent
except for the occasional
siren

Jeanne Morel

But Just a Small Patch of Snow on Mt. Shasta

At the Timbers Inn   Continental Breakfast
scrambled eggs, potatoes, disposable gloves
Red pickup truck with bumper sticker—Keep Bend Blue Collar

    I-5 Southbound.   EXIT NOW   YOU ARE HERE

Count the times firefighters line the side roadside
    yellow jackets / charred embers / hoses

Your foot on the gas

Jeanne Morel

Imbalance

The sand is very hot, the
        water is not that hot in
                the evening the sand is

cold Why should you care ?
        90% them and 10
                % you, it's like that— More

people more cars love so much
        The animal bends water—
                a tricky way to attract

We need some more clarity
        to share in primary school
        It's like that ability

to move in a
        very dry area
                Talk splitting water from salt

Jeanne Morel

Geopolitics

Boramy says
it was so hot yesterday

New Years and 46 years
since the fall of Phnom Penh

here our governor says
they're watching the metrics

Russian Hospital Russian
Roulette—what are the chances?

Jeanne Morel

The Silent Speak As One

Baleen cannot filter the lies, toothless
warm seas that shift beneath bulk.

The wanderer iceberg moans
its crack groan, division.

Failing butterfly wings
in the Amazon quiet winds in Asia.

The wildfires' wisecracks on rain
flare to sky from deaf tree trunks.

The Amur leopards and Siberian tigers
bury cat calls in fallen forests.

The raindrops plash in the fury of storms
no one has seen the likes of before.

The smack of loss that rides the wind
some on scattered sidewalks hear.

Tricia Knoll

EMBERS

Smoke Jumper

As a kid you worked that tin top,
frantic for roar and whine
you hammered at it
til your skinny elbow
almost unsocketed,
red yellow blue green
merging as colorless whir,
as a propeller loses blades
revolving, as thought's obliterated
by engine vibrations en route
to the blaze, remembering how
coach said *don't think,*
crouch padded and clad
impervious to any Fahrenheit,
rigged to ride air, unleashing
calm when the radio says
now borne weightless through branches
and thick shifting black billows, squinting,
grappling, in a temple of devastation,
charred spires skewering massed heat and glare
more blinding than the sharpest
glint you ever saw on cleanest
chrome or most ornate gilt altar,
crane your neck you still can't see an out,
work toward the head,
flank the fire, hack back
underbrush and timber,
pump hard enough
it opens like a lotus
   what
tiny spins inside
     dancer
        jumper
           smoke

                                              Jeanne Julian

Fishflies and Fireworks

Around here mayflies are called fishflies
for the smell they carry with them from the lake.
Electric wings flash in the gas stations' lights
and they fall and die and crunch beneath our tires and the smell reminds us

they are named perfectly.
Even though fishflies don't bite—they don't really have a mouth—
my sister and my son are each afraid of them, of how gently and relentlessly
fishflies rest upon the first surface they find

and die. Looking for some scissors in his desk
I discover Dad's wallet, which must have been among the things
Mom brought back from the hospital after he died. The fishflies
emerge from the lake the same season fireworks burn in the sky, the same season we lost
Dad,

when our noses drip with the closeness of heat and humidity
and our eyes burn with the sun's broad arc, a poor time for a funeral. The fishflies
bring with them Lake St. Clair water and the fire of metamorphosis
and we offer very little in return. We'd expected Dad would come home,

he'd expected it too, and so did the doctors, and so did Mom,
and when Dad called the night before his voice was thin but optimistic.
He listed the procedures and the medicines, the hospital room noisy in the phone,
and when I told him I couldn't hear everything, he said

"Oh, Jason, don't make me say it all again." And that was it.
In Dad's wallet are the usual things: Driver's license, bank card, his list of prescriptions,
scraps of paper with names and phone numbers, his last business card before he retired,
a two-dollar bill for luck. Next summer, kids will play ball again

in the field where Dad coached my sister and me, and fat clouds of fishflies
will rise from their resting spots within the grass and chase the slowest outfielder,
looking for a wall beneath a light where they will wait with patience for what comes next,
leaving behind hardly a suggestion that they once had wings.

                                                Jason Kahler

Desertification

the word desert has no fully agreed upon meaning among geographers
-barry lopez

desertification means a decline in fertility

the something that was is how i'm a woman
the something that was grows / never is

it grows because the world is women
traits pressing down eyelids to close
legs to cross, toes to curl
silence is a seed sown young
they put the words in our mouths
about silence, nail the rules to our backs
take from us the stories of voices
these tongues push up
the back of our teeth til
something else pushes out

the something that was has a life of its own
an aquifer below
                    sapped

Corinne Hughes

Fire in Drought

Q.
She wakes. Smoke. Acrid. Panic, panic
yet it smells of mornings at her old summer camp:
bare knees on earth and damp leaf, kowtowing
to teepeed sticks, peering in to see
ash-tipped twigs blush, glow, and flame,
responsive to her concentrated breath;
and of nighttime bonfires snapping as they flushed
combusting butterflies toward black above,
arabesquing against dark hemlocks then alighting
in the dim-starred sky over the flock of girls
singing sweetly of "Work, Health, Love."

But this may not be safe, *this* reek.
By moonlight her fingers seek
the luminous buttons. She dials shakily.
"Is my house burning, or is it me?"

A.
"It's the brush on Shatterack Mountain.
You can see it coming down the road.
It's moving pretty good. It's pretty
much out of control right now. Problem is,
it's been so dry out here. We pulled out
for the night. It's too dangerous
with all the cliffs. We'll let it burn itself out,
but there'll be hot spots for a while.
Call it bottled genie, bullet
in a chamber, not yet natural disaster.
The fire's cause remains unknown."

Q.
She envisions steaming tangled vines, scorched
moss crusting like loaves, parched
yellow ferns incinerated in a stove

stoked by cauterized limbs, and leaves torched.
White vapor bronze-tinged like a ring
around the moon or gauze on an oozing wound
filters into intervening valleys, singes and rakes
her eyes, gravels her throat like words
she should not say, to him: her secret flint,
her matchbook. But today do they not share
this particulate air, these charred motes?

She wants to kneel, peer within,
to catch his hearth untended, but
there's no invitation. She has her dignity.
"Is it hot in here, or is it me?"

A.
She senses his thoughts hovering like helitack,
choppers tut-tutting, the flash
of pilots' deflective iridescent glasses
as they lower buckets on thick wires
into the river, the machines flying off again
to release harvested drench into wild smoldering acres.
She imagines how with concentrated breath
he doused the candles on his boyhood birthday cakes,
forgetting his wish once the blackened wicks
were exposed and fuming.
She craves enormous rainstorms, saturation.

Jeanne Julian

Heated

A woman finds her husband has been on dating apps. She regrets looking through his iPad. Insomnia is terrible for many reasons. This isn't the first time she's had to find the hammer. Sometimes it's in the junk drawer, sometimes under the sink. She rubs her thumb over its steel head— cold & smooth & hardened like memory. Eight years earlier this woman earned a modest advance for her novel. She used some of the money to buy a MacBook. The day she approved the galleys, she went into labor. Her husband covered his eyes with his Dodgers hat. He couldn't watch. That didn't stop their daughter breaking the amniotic sac. The new mother didn't sleep for months. Before long, she found herself using the hammer on the MacBook— shards of glass & silicon & plastic landing in the creases of the stroller. Her daughter is older now— she watches her mother on the front porch smashing the iPad with a hammer. Father comes home with a new tattoo that spells her mother's name in cursive. As her thumb rubs the bandage, she wonders how much it hurt.

Candice Kelsey

The Kite

On our evening walk we see a kite hanging to the side of our apartment building. The kite's yellow diamond body clings to the shingles and ponders its escape.

We watch with another father son pair as the kite with the yellow diamond body and orange streamers contemplates captivity and freedom.

From the worried look in their eyes, I assume the father son pair are the original owners. The sad face of the son wavers with half tears and half frowns.

The father studies the kite. If he was a sociologist, he would allow the kite to be, yet he is a father with options.

In a country of patriots, it is presumptuous for me to walk away without personifying the kite as a pow coming home to more wars;

its yellow diamond body clipped to shingles; its orange streamers flapping each time a luke-warm breeze entices movement; its entire body disagrees, yet agrees to be disagreeable.

I worry for this kite-not like I worry for my son.
I mean, it's merely a helpless kite.

A yellow and orange kite.
A yellow and orange kite made from paper and string.

A yellow and orange kite without a devil or angle on its deltoids whispering sweet nothings into its ear.

A yellow and orange kite that lacks opposable thumbs and pointer fingers & sleepless nights & toes & knees.

A yellow and orange kite without an anthem & fandom.
A yellow and orange kite made of paper and string without an appetite & palms.

A yellow and orange kite void of organics & goodbye kisses.
A yellow and orange kite made from paper and string codependent on wind & a child (& a father).

A yellow and orange kite not dependent on my metaphors to have
nightmares, Especially when it doesn't sleep.

Durrell Thomson

The Call

My brother winds a spool of black tape
around the frayed cord of the old phone,
tongue curling against lip. His arms
gleam tan, streaked with pale patches
glazed as a snail's path, there
where the fire lit its gasoline torch.
His buddy rolled him in the dirt.
My mother ran for kitchen shears
and sheet, no time to call before
cutting his clothes away, wrapping
her son like a mummy. The nurses
lowered him to cool baths, pulled
the burnt skin off with tweezers,
marked some that was still
good for his back and thighs.

My father knows this space on the edge,
sound gurgling like a bad connection,
damp cellar smell. He too has curled tongue
in the operating room, intent on veins,
on sutures. Now he watches my brother
repair the old rotary, waiting, as he waited,
all those years, for fear-streaked calls,
someone's wife in bathrobe and slippers,
crown rolled with curlers, her man falling
away from earth, from wood, stone and creek,
from her own hands, his face tormented
as an oily rag on the dusty floor of the shop.

He must be ready, my father, for this voice
that comes as nuthatches pull threads
of light through the birch, for this need
no chamomile can calm. The phone
is messenger, his rope about the waist,
a voice he recognizes pulling him
to the man who now hangs on the cliff
like a word that cannot be taken back,
wild huckleberry clinging to gravelly soil,
to whatever mist the sky can spare.

                                                        Carol Barrett

Juggling Two Suns

Dragged up from an early haze. Promoted to shout out loud
brilliance: as if something was fit now for glee, laughter,
now, this precise *life is shite* moment. As if your shine
could be infectious, this brightness, as if it could melt
the day's bedraggle in my soul, right there, in your round
glittery pan. Could you really render
the unsobbed in your fire (and would it yield
charcoal, or ink)? Guarantee simple
celestial damage limitation?

Your strange twin has better ideas, nodding from window after
window, dangling goods with the sagacity of a tricky double:
holding out the late, shabby discounts of this town
as proof. It's saying: see this hurtful cheapness, this rotten
forsaleness, see that? And lets me draw grey conclusions
of my own. It says, repeatedly: I too
come with sparkling promises – but have the grace
to put a price sticker on what I offer. Manageable.
Bite sized hope.

Angela Arnold

Sunset After Brueghel

It's my turn and so Icarus falls
unnoticed, into the algae-
green bottomright.

The plowman
prances behind the ass,
the ship's sail grows
a fat mushroom from the stern.

Ignoring the moon's pull to tide,
the water leaves whole
a rocky pile's outer walls, erect and castle-
like unmoved.

Feathers don't surface.
Sheep pressed head to tail discuss
how the trees remain too bare,
how the clouds coalesce into a creeping
iceberg,

how the sun
is always lower than imagined,
the plump pointing man ignored,
each thrush and wave break
inevitable as a poem.

Jason Kahler

Poets & Acknowledgements

Celia Lisset Alvarez is a writer and educator from Miami, Florida. She holds an MFA in creative writing from the University of Miami and has four collections of poetry, *Shapeshifting* (winner of the 2005 Spire Press Poetry Award), *The Stones* (Finishing Line Press 2006), *Multiverses* (Finishing Line Press 2021), and *Bodies & Words* (Assure Press 2022). Her writing has appeared in numerous journals and anthologies, most recently in *Pink Panther Magazine, DarkWinter Literary Magazine,* and *Last Leaves Magazine*. She has work forthcoming in the anthology *The Book of Life after Death* (Tolsun Books), and in *Blue Mountain Review*. Nominated for both the Pushcart and Best of the Net Prizes, she was the editor of the literary journal *Prospectus: A Literary Offering*. *Multiverses*, a finalist in the narrative poetry category of American Book Fest's Best Books Award, chronicles the loss of her twenty-six-day-old son.

Restrictions was first published in qarrtsiluni, June 12, 2008

Alprentice X Aries is a poet from Michigan and is currently in San Diego studying English literature. He has had his work published in several journals and magazines across the country and abroad including The Beauty Of Black Creations, USC's Social Justice and The Elevation Reviews. Alprentice X Aries believes in your voice, your choice, and your freedom of life.

Angela Arnold's poems have been published in a variety of UK poetry magazines as well as online. They have also been included in anthologies produced by Templar, Frogmore Press, Eyewear and others. Her collection *In/Between* is coming out next year (Stairwell Books). She is also an artist and a creative gardener who enjoys her synaesthesia and language/s and is currently learning Welsh. @AngelaArnold777

Constance Bacchus currently lives with her daughter in the Pacific Northwest. Her work can be found in or is forthcoming in places like *Cirque Journal, Icefloe Press, Permafrost Magazine, Blue River Review, Sand* and *NoD*. Her book *sound like you* was created by Red Mare Press this year. Recently she won an award from Yakima Coffeehouse Poets Annual Poetry Contest.

Devon Balwit walks in all weather. Her most recent collections are *Rubbing Shoulders with the Greats* [Seven Kitchens Press 2020] and *Dog-Walking in the Shadow of Pyongyang* [Nixes Mate Books, 2021]
pelapdx.wixsite.com/devonbalwitpoet

Carol Barrett holds doctorates in Creative Writing and Clinical Psychology. She coordinates the Creative Writing Certificate program for doctoral students in Interdisciplinary Studies at Union Institute & University. Carol has published two volumes of poetry, including *Calling in the Bones*, which won the Snyder Prize from Ashland Poetry Press, and one of creative nonfiction, *Pansies*, a finalist for the Oregon Book Awards. Her poems have appeared in *JAMA, The Women's Review of Books, Poet Lore, Poetry International,* and *Nimrod*, as well as several magazines in Britain, Haiti and Canada. She has also published research articles in psychology, women's studies, religious studies, education, and dance and art therapy journals. The recipient of a Poetry Fellowship from the National Endowment for the Arts, Carol has lived in nine states of the US and in England. She attended the coronation of Queen Elizabeth II as a toddler.

Lessons for Fifty Cents was first published in Cottonwood Review, volume 22, 1980.
The Call was first published in Falling Star Magazine, Summer issue, 2018.
The Tempering was first published in Cirque, volume 8(2), 2017.

Ahimsa Timoteo Bodhrán is the author of *Archipiélagos*, *Antes y después del Bronx: Lenapehoking*, and *South Bronx Breathing Lessons*; editor of the international queer Indigenous issue of *Yellow Medicine Review: A Journal of Indigenous Literature, Art, and Thought*; and co-editor of the Native dance/movement/performance issue of *Movement Research Performance Journal*. He recently organized the world's first transgender Arab roundtable dialogue for *Sinister Wisdom: A Multicultural Lesbian Literary & Art Journal*. He has received scholarships/fellowships from CantoMundo, Macondo, Radius of Arab American Writers, Voices of Our Nations Arts Foundation, and Lambda Literary. His work appears in Ireland in *Channel, The Galway Review, The Ogham Stone, Revival, ROPES,* and *The SHOp*; Northern Ireland in *A New Ulster*; Scotland in *Markings, Read This, The Red Wheelbarrow,* and *Reliquiae*; Wales in *Envoi* and *Poetry Wales*; and England in *Brand, the deliquents, Fuselit, Iota, Magma, Other Poetry, Poetry Review, Polluto, Sable, Trespass,* and *Weyfarers*.

"Wind" was previously published in *Markings*, Issue 29, in 2009.
"Hummingbirds in the Forest of Needle and Blood" was previously published in *1110*, Issue 10, in 2016.

Sharon Dornberg-Lee's poetry has appeared in Literary Mama; Sow's Ear Poetry Review; Mamas and Papas; Politics/Letters, Car Poems: A Collective Vehicle; Earth's Daughters, and Rust Belt Chicago. Her essay, Cold Turkey on Big Bird, was featured on the Chicago Public Radio program 848 and she was featured on WBEZ's Dynamic Range. Sharon is the manager of CJE SeniorLife's counseling program and she has been an adjunct instructor at the University of Chicago Crown School of Social Work, Policy and Practice. She currently teaches in Crown's Professional Development Program. Sharon lives in Chicago with her husband; their daughter, Sophie, just graduated from NYU.

Kris Falcon's poems are forthcoming or have appeared in *Atlanta Review, Great River Review, filling Station, Gulf Stream Magazine, Red Rock Review,* and elsewhere. She has been nominated for the Pushcart Prize. She is the author of *Alunsina's Wrist*. She has a forthcoming poetry collection, *Some Blue, a Little Spur*. She holds an MFA at the School of the Art Institute of Chicago.

Alexis Rhone Fancher is published in *Best American Poetry, Rattle, Verse Daily, The American Journal of Poetry, Plume, Diode, Spillway, Nashville Review* and elsewhere. She's authored seven poetry collections, most recently, *Junkie Wife (Moon Tide Press), The Dead Kid Poems (KYSO Flash Press), DUETS (Small Harbor Editions) and EROTIC: New & Selected (NYQ Books)*. Her next book, *BRAZEN,* again from *NYQ Books*, publishes in early 2023. Her photographs are featured worldwide, including the covers of *Pithead Chapel, Witness, The Pedestal Magazine,* and *The Chiron Review*. A coffee table book of her photos of Los Angeles poets publishes in 2023 from Moon Tide Press. A multiple Pushcart Prize and Best of the Net nominee, Alexis is poetry editor of *Cultural Daily* since 2012. She lives with her husband on the bluffs of San Pedro, overlooking the Pacific Ocean, just a stone's throw from downtown Los Angeles. They have an extraordinary view. www.alexisrhonefancher.com

We carry our identity on our fingertips was originally published in "The Night Heron Barks" - 2020

Patrick Cabello Hansel is the author of the poetry collections *The Devouring Land* (Main Street Rag Publishing) and *Quitting Time* (Atmosphere Press) and the forthcoming *Breathing in Minneapolis* (Finishing Line Press). He has published poems and prose in over 85 journals, including *Crannog, Ilanot Review, Hawai'i Pacific Review, Ash & Bones, RiverSedge* and *Lunch Ticket,* and won awards from the Loft Literary Center and MN State Arts Board. His novella *Searching* was serialized in 33 issues of *The Alley News*. He is the editor of *The Phoenix of Phillips*, a literary journal by and for the most diverse community in Minneapolis. He has taught creative writing in elementary and high schools, and with seniors and 1st generation immigrants. His website is: www.artecabellohansel.com

Nicole Arocho Hernández grew up in Cabo Rojo, Puerto Rico. Her poems have been published in The Acentos Review, Electric Literature, The Academy of American Poets, and elsewhere. Her first chapbook, *I Have No Ocean,* was published online with Sundress Publications. Her second chapbook is forthcoming with Glass Poetry Press. She is the Translations Editor at Hayden's Ferry Review and an MFA candidate at Arizona State University.

Janis Butler Holm served as Associate Editor for *Wide Angle*, the film journal, and currently works as a writer and editor in sunny Los Angeles. Her prose, poems, and performance pieces have appeared in small-press, national, and international magazines. Her plays have been produced in the U.S., Canada, Russia, and the U.K.

Corinne Hughes is a queer American poet and fiction writer. Her work has been supported by Tin House and the National Book Foundation. Her poetry can be found in *Passengers Journal, Cathexis Northwest Press, Cirque Journal, Grim and Gilded*, and is forthcoming in the *Horror Writers Association Poetry Showcase IX*. She currently serves as a poetry reader for *Palette Poetry* and studies in the Poets Studio at the Attic Institute in Portland, Oregon, where she lives with her two blue Finnish gerbils.

Thomas Irvine holds a BA in English and American Literature from the University of Leicester, and an MA in Poetry from the University of East Anglia. He currently works as Publicity and Marketing Executive for British Library Publishing and co-runs a spoken-word charity in Hertfordshire called 'Shout or Whisper'.

Jeanne Julian is the author of *Like the O in Hope* (The Poetry Box, 2019) and two chapbooks. Her poems appear in *Poetry Quarterly, Red Fez, Bacopa Literary Review, Snapdragon, Kakalak, Ocotillo Review,* and other journals and have won awards from *Reed Magazine, The Comstock Review, Naugatuck River Review*, and Maine Poets' Society. She regularly reviews poetry books for *The Main Street Rag*. Jeanne lives in South Portland, Maine and helps to coordinate the Nexus Poets open mic in New Bern, NC. www.jeannejulian.com

Smoke Jumper was first published in Flying South 2019.

Jason Kahler is a teacher, writer, and scholar from Southeast Michigan. His work has appeared in *Analog, Seneca Review,* the *Journal of Contemporary Criminal Justice*, the *Stonecoast Review*, and other scholarly and literary publications. His poem "Walls, Stars, Eyes, Walls" earned a Best of the Net nomination. You're welcome to tweet him @JasonKahler3.

Sunset After Brueghel was first published in Arsenic Lobster, Spring, 2007.

Lisa Kamolnick is a poet and photographer whose work explores human nature, the human condition, the natural world, and what lies between and beyond. After a nomadic military childhood, Lisa planted herself in the sugar-white sands of northwest Florida beaches and later traced an ancestral trail to northeast Tennessee's highlands. She holds a B.A. in English from University of Florida. Her works have appeared or are forthcoming in such publications as *HeartWood Literary Magazine, Women Speak, Vol. 7, Black Moon Magazine, Tennessee Voices*, and *Wild Roof Journal*. Learn more at lisakamolnick.com

Lisa Namdar Kaufman is a writer, filmmaker, and translator. Her written work has appeared in *Quarterly West, West Wind Review, MARGIE: Journal of American*

Poetry, and *McSweeney's Internet Tendency*, among others. Her short films have won awards and appeared in festivals around the world from Cannes to Hong Kong. Lisa laughs too loud, lingers too long in the garden, and doesn't move nearly enough but maybe someday she will become a dancer. In the meantime, she is working on her first book-length poetry collection. She teaches screenwriting and holds a BA from Brown University and an MFA in film from Columbia University.

Candice Kelsey [she/her] is a poet, educator, and activist currently living in Augusta, Georgia. She serves as a creative writing mentor with PEN America's Prison & Justice Writing Program; her work appears in Grub Street, Poet Lore, Lumiere Review, Hawai'i Pacific Review, and Slant among other journals. Recently, Candice was chosen as a finalist in Iowa Review's Poetry Contest and Cutthroat's Joy Harjo Poetry Prize. Her third book titled A Poet just released with Alien Buddha Press. Find her @candicekelsey1 and www.candicemkelseypoet.com.

Tricia Knoll knows the edges of silence and speech. She is a Vermont poet with a speech disability that gives an edginess to her readings. She lives alone in a second-growth forest. Much of her work is eco-poetry – *One Bent Twig* coming from Future Cycle Press in 2023 sings to trees caught in climate change and history as well as her own history with trees. *Let's Hear It for the Horses* (2022) offers poems for the love of horses. In 2018 *How I Learned To Be White* received the Human Relations Indie Book Award for Motivational Poetry. *Ocean's Laughter* recorded change over time in Manzanita, a small town on Oregon's north coast. Knoll is a Contributing Editor to Verse Virtual. Website: triciaknoll.com

Peggy Landsman is the author of the full-length poetry collection, *Too Much World, Not Enough Chocolate* (forthcoming from Nightingale & Sparrow Press, 2023), and two poetry chapbooks, *Our Words, Our Worlds* (Kelsay Books, 2021) and *To-wit To-woo* (Foothills Publishing, 2008). She lives in South Florida where she swims in the warm Atlantic Ocean every chance she gets. A selection of her poetry and prose can be read on her website: https://peggylandsman.wordpress.com/

Ecce Femina was first published in RED OWL MAGAZINE, Issue XXIV, 2007

Gail Langstroth is a tri-lingual lecturer, international eurythmy performer, translator, poet and film artist. She is a graduate of Drew University's M.F.A. in poetry and winner of the Patricia Dobler Poetry Prize, 2011. Get Fresh Books released Langstroth's bilingual *firegarden / jardín-de-fuego,* (2020). *Voiced: words from asphalt,* Langstroth's 2021 film, was showcased in European festivals. STAHLWORTE / STEELWORDS, Langstroth's 9-part performance piece premiered in The Netherlands, (October 2021). In February (2023) she returns to Germany for performances and *Before Now / After I* an exhibition of her visual art which opens on the 9th in Hamburg. www.wordmoves.com

Olivia Lee is a poet, novelist, playwright, and English professor. She has published two novels. Her poetry has been published in DoveTales—Writing for Peace, Sonnets for Shakespeare, Haunted Waters Press, Wild Roof Journal, HerStry, and the Closed Eye Open, among others. Her play, In Emma Rendell's Attic, had a pre-pandemic stage reading. She is committed to social justice work and supporting Fair Trade companies. She enjoys books, art, travel, listening to music, walking in the woods, and spending time with her sister, Suzie, and their two dogs, George MacDonald and Keeper Lee. Connect: instagram@ladyolivialee

Christina Lovin's prose and poetry has appeared in over one hundred literary journals and anthologies in the U.S., as well as abroad. She has published six volumes of poetry (Echo, A Stirring in the Dark, God of Sparrows, Flesh, Little Fires, and What We Burned for Warmth). Lovin is the recipient of numerous poetry awards, writing residencies, fellowships, and grants, most notably the AWP Kurt Brown Scholarship, the Al Smith Fellowship from Kentucky Arts Council, Kentucky Foundation for Women Artist Enrichment Grants, and an Elizabeth George Foundation Grant. A native Illinoisan, Lovin currently teaches writing full-time in Central Kentucky, where she is accessory faculty in the Bluegrass Writers Studio, the MFA program at Eastern Kentucky University.

The Poet gets Advice from Tom Wolfe at Toscanini's Ice Cream Shop and *CLUB PARADISE Lost* were first Published in Stimulus Respond (UK)
Burning the Love Letters was first published in Levue Littéraire, France

Joshua Moncure is a non-binary writer, poet, and musician raised and currently residing in Kansas City. Josh wields a fiery passion for written poetry as well as the spoken word, but when Josh isn't creating they bartend and DJ at nightclubs in Kansas City. Josh's work explores the unconscious and lived experience of black individuals birthed and raised in the United States. Josh is the child of two doctors and grew up with 3 siblings. The first 18 years of Josh's life was lived in a vast majority white neighborhood, and Josh's work hopes to resonate with black people who experience the suffocation of living in places where their blackness is taught and expected to be muted. Read more of Josh's work at runpoetrun.com

Jeanne Morel is the author of the chapbooks, "I See My Way to Some Partial Results" (Ravenna Press); "Jackpot" (Bottlecap Press); and "That Crossing Is Not Automatic" (Tarpaulin Sky Press). Her recent poems have appeared or are forthcoming in The Dodge, Great Weather for MEDIA, and Blue Earth Review. Her poem "Loss & Other Forms of Death" won the 2021 Fugue Poetry Prize. Jeanne lives in Seattle and teaches writing at Seattle Central College.

Robbi Nester lives and writes in Southern California. She is the author of four books of poetry and editor of three anthologies. Her poetry and reviews have appeared widely. Learn more at: www.robbinester.net.

Emmy Newman's work has appeared or is forthcoming in *Poetry Northwest CALYX: A Journal, New Ohio Review, Yemassee,* and elsewhere. She has been nominated for Best New Poets, several Pushcart Prizes, and was a finalist for Best of the Net 2022. Find her on Instagram @she_wins_an_emmy.

Hell Planet was first published in *Night Coffee,* Issue 1, Spring 2021
If French Kissing Was as Good a Promised Shouldn't I be Happy by Now? was first published in *New Ohio Review,* Issue 31, February 2020

Saleem Hue Penny (him/friend) is a Black disabled "rural hip hop blues" poet who punctuates his work with drum loops, field sounds, gouache and birch bark. He is the 2021 Poetry Coalition Fellow at Zoeglossia, an Assistant Poetry Editor at Bellevue Literary Revue, a member of Obsidian's inaugural "O|Session Black Listening" 2022 cohort and a proud Cave Canem Fellow. Learn more at: saleemhue.me

Daniel Peralta received his bachelor's degree in English literature from the University of Tennessee Chattanooga. He currently resides in Wisconsin with his wife, his son, and two cats. In his free time, he likes playing cards, board games, attending Lorde concerts, and playing the piano. This is his first publication.

MK PUNKY is the author of 13 books of fiction, journalism, and memoir, and the creator of the multi-media museum exhibition "The Year of When," featuring 365-poems. MK serves as poet laureate of Vista Street Community library in Los Angeles.

Laura Ann Reed, a San Francisco Bay Area native, taught modern dance and ballet at the University of California, Berkeley before working as a leadership development trainer at the San Francisco headquarters of the United States Environmental Protection Agency. She and her husband now reside in western Washington. Her work has been anthologized in *How To Love the World,* and is forthcoming in 2023 in the *Storey Publishing* anthology, *The Wonder of Small Things,* edited by James Crews. Her poems have appeared in *ONE ART, Willawaw, Loch Raven, Swwim* and *The Ekphrastic Review,* among other journals. Her chapbook, *Shadows Thrown,* is slated for publication in spring, 2023.

How I Want to be Wanted was first published by *The Ekphrastic Review* in Spring 2022

Stephanie Staab is an American poet living in the Black Forest, Germany. Her poetry has appeared or is forthcoming in Lake Effect, Lunch Ticket, Crab Creek Review and Chestnut Review among others. Her second chapbook, Letterlocking, is forthcoming from Alternating Current Press.

Suspicion was first published in Chiron Review, Issue #121, Spring 2021.

Alex Starr is a writer in the San Francisco Bay Area. Alex's poems have been published in *Vallum: Contemporary Poetry, Atlas & Alice, Snapdragon Journal, The Literary Bohemian, Lunch Ticket, Zoetic Press, The Write Launch,* and *Meat for Tea: The Valley Review.* Prior recognitions include the Dorothy Sugarman Prize in Poetry, George Harmon Coxe Award in Fiction, and Barnes Shakespeare Essay Prize from the Cornell University English Department. Alex holds a B.A. in Philosophy/English from Cornell and Oxford where he co-led the Mansfield College Poetry Society.

Cassie Premo Steele PhD, is an award-winning, eco-feminist author or 16 books and audio programs ranging from novels to poetry, nonfiction and scholarship. These include *The ReSisters, We Heal from Memory* and nonfiction book, *Earth Joy Writing,* published by Ashland Creek Publishing in Oregon, available at Congaree National Park, where she leads seasonal forest journaling workshops. Her chapbook *Swimming in Gilead* is forthcoming from Yellow Arrow Publishing. Her poetry has won numerous awards, including the Archibald Rutledge Prize named after the first Poet Laureate of South Carolina, where she lives with her wife.

Jennifer Thal is twenty-seven-year-old Philadelphian transplant in Chicago pursuing a doctorate in clinical psychology. Her work has appeared on The Esthetic Apostle, Typishly, and Haunted Waters Press. She enjoys reading at open mic nights, advocating for body acceptance and positivity, and empowering her readers through her writing.

Durell Thompson is a student, teacher, father, husband, and son. Through his poetry, he looks to explore the multifaceted connections that define the African American experience in the United States. Moreover, he uses his poetry as a way to embrace his roles as an educator, writer, and father, and to prepare his son to live and thrive as a black man. Works from Durell Thompson have appeared in Bayou Magazine ('Black Son'), Beacon (SHSU review) ('Welfare Line', 'Bilingual Waitress', 'Watermelon Lady', and 'My view on Clouds (ode to "Darius and the Clouds")'

t.m. thomson has had 3 of her poems nominated for Pushcart Awards. She is co-author of *Frame and Mount the Sky* (2017) and author of *Strum and Lull* (2019), which placed in Golden Walkman's 2017 chapbook competition, and *The Profusion* (2019). Her first full-length collection, *Plunge,* will be published in 2022. Her passions include kickboxing, playing in mud, and savoring art. You can find her at: www.facebook.com/TaunjaThomsonWriter/.

Ellen June Wright was born in Bedford, England but currently lives in New Jersey. Her poems have appeared or are forthcoming in *Naugatuck River Review, New York Quarterly, Plume, Atlanta Review, River Mouth Review, Santa Fe Writers Project, Solstice, The Elevation Review, Paterson Literary Review, The Caribbean Writer, Obsidian: Literature & Arts in the African Diaspora* and elsewhere. She is a

Cave Canem and Hurston/Wright alumna. She received five 2021 Pushcart Prize Nominations for poetry. When she is not writing, she enjoys crocheting, swimming and watching British crime dramas. You may follow her on twitter @EllenJuneWrites.

www.blacksunflowerspoetry.com

www.ingramcontent.com/pod-product-compliance
Lightning Source LLC
Chambersburg PA
CBHW051331110526
44590CB00032B/4484